VERDICTS
AND
HOLES

The Trail of the Anti-Trump Conspiracy
and the Mueller Investigation

Book 2 of "IN SPITE OF THEM"

Janvier T. Chando

PUBLISHED BY TISI BOOKS
www.tisibooks.com

NEW YORK, RALEIGH, LONDON, AMSTERDAM

ISBN-13: 978-1-0872-0992-0
ISBN-10: 1-0872-0992-7

PUBLISHED BY TISI BOOKS

www.tisibooks.com

NEW YORK, RALEIGH, LONDON, AMSTERDAM

Printed in The United States of America

Non-Fiction Titles by Janvier T.Chando

IN SPITE OF THEM: The Two-Term Presidency of Donald Trump
FALLEN HEROES: African Leaders Whose Assassinations…
UKRAINE: The Tug-of-War Between Russia and the West
THE CANARY IN A COAL MINE EFFECT:…
Cameroon: The Haunted Heart of Africa

Fiction Titles by Janvier Chando

The Usurper: and Other Stories
Triple Agent, Double Cross
Disciples of Fortune
The Union Moujik
Flash of the Sun
Fortune Calls
Fortune's Master
Fortune's Children
The Norilsk Bears
To Be In Love and To Be Wise
The Fire and Ice Legend
The Sweetest Madness
The Grandmothers
The Hunger Fire
The Shades of Fire
Father and Sons
The Doctor
Dark Shades
Fateful Ties
The Verdict of Hades
His Majesty's Trial
Ngoko's Folly
The Usurper
The Dowry
I am Hated
The Oaf

Upcoming Titles by Janvier Chando

The White Falcon
The Drift at Home
The Mortal Friends

DEDICATION

This book is dedicated to Anna M. Chitja, Dr. Samuel F. Tchwenko, Christopher N. Chando

ACKNOWLEDGEMENTS

My deepest, warmest and everlasting thanks to Salomon
Muna Yakana, Macdonald Chanda, Emos Mbiatom

Contents

VERDICTS
AND
HOLES

Book II of "IN SPITE OF THEM"

Quotes

"We find that at present the human race is divided into one wise man, nine knaves, and ninety fools out of every hundred. That is, by an optimistic observer. The nine knaves assemble themselves under the banner of the most knavish among them, and become 'politicians'; the wise man stands out, because he knows himself to be hopelessly outnumbered, and devotes himself to poetry, mathematics, or philosophy; while the ninety fools plod off under the banners of the nine villains, according to fancy, into the labyrinths of chicanery, malice and warfare. It is pleasant to have command, observes Sancho Panza, even over a flock of sheep, and that is why the politicians raise their banners. It is, moreover, the same thing for the sheep whatever the banner. If it is democracy, then the nine knaves will become members of parliament; if fascism, they will become party leaders; if communism, commissars. Nothing will be different, except the name. The fools will be still fools, the knaves still leaders, the results still exploitation. As for the wise man, his lot will be much the same under any ideology. Under democracy he will be encouraged to starve to death in a garret, under fascism he will be put in a concentration camp, under communism he will be liquidated."

T.H. White

"Remember, remember always, that all of us, and you and I especially, are descended from immigrants and revolutionists."

Franklin D. Roosevelt

"We are in the process of creating what deserves to be called the idiot culture. Not an idiot sub-culture, which every society has bubbling beneath the surface and which can provide harmless fun; but the culture itself. For the first time, the weird and the stupid and the coarse are becoming our cultural norm, even our cultural ideal."
Carl Bernstein

"If you want to make peace with your enemy, you have to work with your enemy. Then he becomes your partner."
Nelson Mandela

"Here's to the crazy ones. The misfits. The rebels. The troublemakers. The round pegs in the square holes. The ones who see things differently. They're not fond of rules. And they have no respect for the status quo. You can quote them, disagree with them, glorify or vilify them. About the only thing you can't do is ignore them. Because they change things. They push the human race forward. And while some may see them as the crazy ones, we see genius. Because the people who are crazy enough to think they can change the world, are the ones who do."
Rob Siltanen

"Never compete with someone who has nothing to lose."
Baltasar Gracian

"Mankind must put an end to war before war puts an end to mankind."
John F. Kennedy

"The darkest places in hell are reserved for those who maintain their neutrality in times of moral crisis."
Dante Alighieri

"The most dangerous man, to any government, is the man who is able to think things out for himself without regard to the prevailing superstitions and taboos. Almost inevitably he comes to the conclusion that the government he lives under is dishonest, insane and intolerable, and so, if he is romantic, he tries to change it. And even if he is not romantic personally he is apt to spread discontent among those who are."

H.L. Mencken

"In the end, you're measured not by how much you undertake but by what you finally accomplish."

Donald Trump

"Live as if you were to die tomorrow. Learn as if you were to live forever."

Mahatma Gandhi

"Everything we hear is an opinion, not a fact. Everything we see is a perspective, not the truth."

Marcus Aurelius

"I have never let my schooling interfere with my education."

Mark Twain

"...The world gets blessed every now and then with unique souls who though burdened by their invisible crosses, still have the extraordinary strength to forge ahead in life and give others a helping hand at the same time. Despite their tribulations, most of us think they are fine. Even when the weight of their crosses becomes unbearable, even when they proceed in a breathless manner, we still have a hard time understanding that they are drowning. In fact, we even condemn them for failing to sacrifice more..."

Janvier Chouteu-Chando, Disciples of Fortune

"It is not the person with a lot of money that is happy. It is the person with enough money that easily finds happiness."
Alexander Zakharchenko

"You educate a man; you educate a man. You educate a woman; you educate a generation."
Brigham Young

Maps

Map of the USA

2008 Presidential Election Map

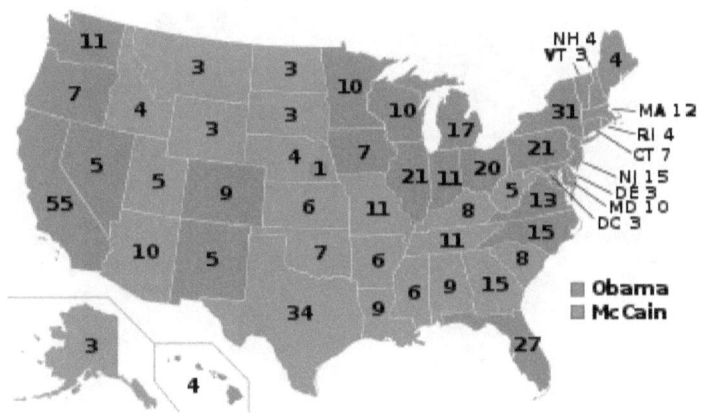

2012 Presidential Election Map

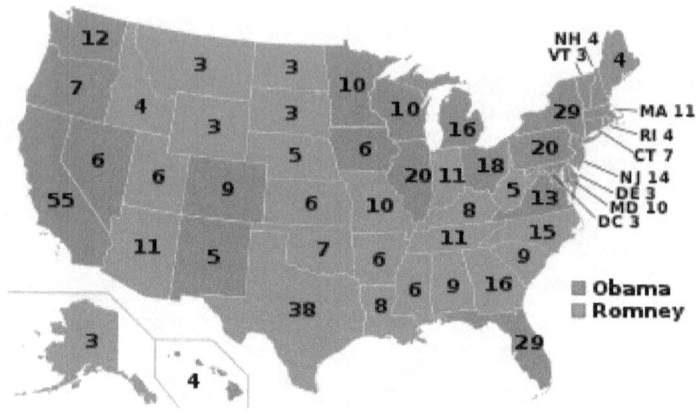

2016 Presidential Election Map

Democratic Party
Republican Party
Libertarian Party
Green Party
Constitution Party

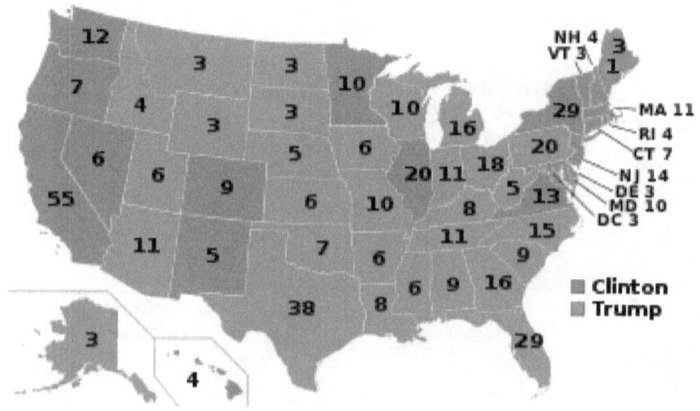

Summary of results of the 2004-2016 presidential elections

States carried by the Republicans in all four elections
States carried by the Republicans in three of the four elections
States carried by each party twice in the four elections
States carried by the Democrats in three of the four elections
States carried by the Democrats in all four elections

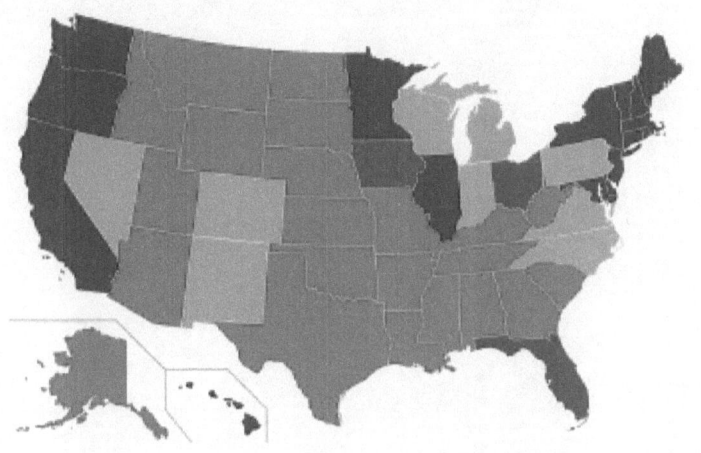

Introduction

It is more than two and a half years since the inauguration of the renowned businessman and television personality Donald John Trump as the 45th and current President of the United States of America following his upset win against Hillary Rodham Clinton, the nominee of the Democratic Party in the 2016 presidential election. The colorfulness of that race etched on the memories of most Americans and a large number of citizens of other countries of the world more than any other presidential election before it. Donald Trump's electoral triumph was the culmination of a fascinating campaign all right, with the Republican Party primaries serving as a teaser where he emerged victorious against a long line of thirteen contenders, and then went on to clinch the Republican Party nomination.

Verdicts and Holes is an account of what is considered by many to be the most embarrassing political circus experienced by the United States of America in over half a century. If the story of Russian Interference in the 2016 US. Presidential election, and of allegations that Donald Trump's campaign colluded with Russia to secure a victory for him against the highly-rated Hillary Clinton was intended to prevent a US. rapprochement with Russian, then it served its purpose in the short term; if the intention was to strengthen the political establishment, the outcome of the Special Counsel investigation proved that the narrative resulted in more questions than answers, and that it created a platform that could see the investigators getting investigated.

However, it is not only elements of the bureaucracy that have experienced pitfalls recently. The past three years have exposed the Western mainstream media to self-censorship, as more and more people come to understand its powerful role in creating narratives and consensus, in creating doubletalk and in contributing to the wreckage of press freedom in a manner that some pundits are even comparing to the days of the Soviet Union when impartial and independent thinking was lacking, where propaganda was churned out daily as news; when censorship was the norm and when make-beliefs driven by an ideology of utopia reigned supreme. However, unlike in the days of the Communist East and the Union of Soviet Socialist Republics (USSR) or the Soviet Union where the media was used to prop up the ideology, the system and the undemocratic government; the Western corporate media dominated by the left-wing communication outlets, churn out news and information that undermines the Trump administration, and strengthens the bureaucracy and the political establishment for a purpose that only very few people can fathom.

The purpose of *Verdicts and Holes*, which in essence is Book 2 of the enlightening and groundbreaking book *IN SPITE OF THEM: The Two-Term Presidency of Donald Trump*, is to provide a clear and coherent picture of the story that arose from the allegation that the Trump campaign colluded with Russia to win the 2016 presidential election. It is also a journey into the casualties of the Mueller investigation and those vindicated in what the president calls a witch-hunt. Hopefully, this account provides lessons that would help the governed and the governing in the United States of America, as well as the media that is supposed to assist them, play their roles for the welfare of the country; hopefully this account helps in creating a better understanding between all the competing factions in American society, in the government, and in the US. economy.

We find at the end of this account that we have been provided with the resources to come to our own conclusions in determining whether the claim by the initiators and supporters of the Mueller Investigation that the Trump-Russia collusion narrative itself was not the crime, but that the 'cover-up' is, is true; or whether the whole inquiry was a witch-hunt that that failed to serve all its purpose.

Prolegomenon

The atypical nature of Donald Trump's presidency dominated the conversations of most families and friends that gathered together to break bread or to toast drinks at their homes, eateries, bars and other public places during the major holidays. However, if in 2016 and the better part of 2017, the topic of discussion was on how the businessman and television star won the 2016 presidential election, rattled the political establishment, mortified the mainstream media and awed if not stunned most Americans and the majority of the informed people of the world, the exchanges today have become more reflective, sober, grim and uncompromising, reflecting the polarizing nature of politics today, especially in the United States of America.

The current nature of politics in the country is a reflection of the apparent hardening of the opinions, beliefs, and positions of the two mainstream political parties, developments that the populations supporting them or their points of view tend to amplify.

Discussions, conversations, arguments, counsels and debates these days tend to be more about Donald J. Trump's logic-defying presidency — the inability to pin the

45th president down on the numerous claims or allegations made against him; the so-called increased polarization of American society at a time that he is winning more support from the country's racial minorities; the alienation of America's traditional allies abroad at a time that he is getting them more involved in the working and financing of NATO (North Atlantic Treaty Organization), which is the intergovernmental military alliance between 29 countries in North America and Europe; the United States of America's economic and trade wars not only with America's adversaries, but also with its allies and partners; the president's apparent penchant to pull the USA out of economic and military deals the superpower had made with other countries, especially when he judges that these treaties no longer serve America's interests, et cetera et cetera.

The task of a pundit trying to find rational answers to the turmoil in the country's socio-economic and political life arising from the blind and calculated actions of both the Trump camp and those opposing his person and his politics, starts with understanding the promises the president made, especially after he clinched the Republican Party nomination, and then went on to pledge in a more vigorous manner during the election campaign to "Make America Great Again"…

As Donald Trump anchors himself in the second half of his first term in office and starts positioning himself for another term, developments will show that his command of the highest office of the land could be more beneficial for the country than expected, as the conflicting forces in

America come to terms with the reality of his presidency and as he too adjusts to the reality of consensus in decision-making by seeking common grounds with the judiciary and the legislative branches of government. The outcome of these unavoidable compromises from both the Trump camp and the camp of those who are opposed to or are lukewarm about the Trump presidency, promises to make the next eighteen months and potentially the next six years very colorful indeed.

CHAPTER ONE

The Salamander

"Two things are infinite: the universe and human stupidity; and I'm not sure about the universe."
Albert Einstein

"The best thing to give to your enemy is forgiveness; to an opponent, tolerance; to a friend, your heart; to your child, a good example; to a father, deference; to your mother, conduct that will make her proud of you; to yourself, respect; to all others, charity."
Benjamin Franklin

"The enemy is not the one who is facing you with a sword in hand, that's the opponent. The enemy is the one behind you with a knife at your back."
Thomas Sankara

People, and more especially the category of Americans

whose loyalty to anyone or to any entity hinges on the personal benefits they derive from having a relationship with that person or body, have a hard time understanding the nature of Donald Trump's support base. The disconnect can be traced way back, even before the start of his presidency, when many pundits and analysts of different shades first tried to elaborate on the rationale for the 35 percent solid support that the president had been commanding among the electorate since his election into the Oval Office, as if everything depends on empirical formulas. However, the past two and a half years have exposed several flaws in the analyses postulated by some of these gurus or savants on the nature of Donald Trump's core supporters.

How does one then explain the fact that the Republican Party which traditionally catered for the interest of the wealthy class and which drew much of its support from the country's deeply religious, is having a billionaire Republican in the White House who nevertheless commands the support of a medley range of Americans that Hillary Clinton described as a "Basket of Deplorables", the majority of whom are economically underprivileged, yet constitute the group that has the highest percentage of his core supporters?

The fact that this category of Americans rose from 35 percent in early 2017 to 36 percent in April 2019, with the increase coming from all the racial groups in the country, presents an intriguing angle for any gung-ho analysts.

We don't have to think deeply or look far to figure out why many people find that increase among Donald

Trump's core supporters intriguing. The anticipation that accompanied the 2018-2019 shutdown when most of his opponents and even some of those who were not really against him thought that the standoff between Republicans and Democrats in Congress over funding for the president's proposed border wall would shrink the size of his core supporters, was grounded on solid analysis. However, the opposition's expectations of political gains from that hiccup turned out to be a pyrrhic victory only. All the different polls taken since January 2019 show a consistent drop in the percentage of Americans who disapprove of Donald Trump's presidency, a decline that has been steady to the point where the president's core support base has risen to 36 percent of adult Americans.

Trump Administration's 2019 Approval Rating

Company/Monthly Percentages	January 2019	February 2019	March 2019	April 2019	May 2019
Ipsos (for Reuters)	39%	41%	42%	39%	39%
YouGov (for The Economist)	37%	40%	43%	42%	42%
Investor's Business Daily	42%	39%	41%	41%	43%
NBC News/Wall Street Journal	43%	46%	53%		46%
Gallup	37%	43%	39%	46%	

There are certain things, certain people and certain situations that the well-informed mind has a hard time fathoming. Donald Trump happens to be one of them. So much dirt has been flung at him that his approval ratings should have plummeted to the point where we should be expecting him to suffer a humiliating loss in the 2020 presidential election with a lower percentage or vote count than even Jimmy Carter, who as an incumbent, lost the 1984 Presidential Election by 41% (35,480,115) to Ronald Reagan's 50.7% (43,903,230). It is as if the American people, or more specifically Donald Trump's core supporters, have come to the conclusion that American politics, like that of many other countries dominated by powerful interest groups, is replete with intrigues, conspiracies, make-beliefs, and secret plans; it is as if they are seeing something of Machiavelli in those opposing the 45th president and so are reacting to it instinctively and calculatingly by distrusting the mainstream media that harps on allegations, many of which are baseless, that the president colluded with Russia, obstructed justice, etc.

Donald Trump's core supporters distrust the bureaucracy made up of cabinet departments, government corporations, independent agencies, and regulatory commissions; they wonder about the bureaucracy that sees the United States of America as the world's only military, economic and diplomatic superpower and seems determined to do whatever it takes to continue leading the world. The corporate media and the bureaucracy have become less attractive to the majority of these Trump core supporters since he started regulating American affairs from the Oval Office.

It would be wrong to say that there is no truth in all the accusations that have been made against the 45th US. president, or that he does not deserve all the dirt that has been thrown at him. The United States of America's first gentleman has an abrasive personality among other things, which is why it would surprise nobody that he has irked some of the people he crossed paths with. And based on a scorecard of scandals and allegations against him, it is easy to conclude that he is attracted to actions that many consider morally wrong and borderline legal, while having strong immunity against them at the same time. I say so because Donald Trump has put up an ambivalent defense to the accusations heaped on him by his opponents calling to question his pledge to "Drain the Swamp" in Washington DC, yet he seems unscathed by these charges or claims.

If not:

- then how can one explain the failure to provide damaging information or the sudden quietness about the entanglements involving Donald Trump's family, his businesses and his presidency, especially the much-talked-about Trump Organization which he has not divested from, a lucrative business per se that generated at least $500 million in revenue in 2017 and $479 million in 2018?

- what is the explanation for the fizzling out of the defamation lawsuit by 15 women who claimed he sexually assaulted them?

- how does one explain the crumbling of the allegation by the former porn star Stormy Daniels (real name Stephanie Clifford) that she had an affair with the then president-to-be in 2006 and that Donald Trump's lawyer Michael Cohen paid her the sum of $130,000 to be quiet about it ahead of the 2016 presidential election, an action that is considered a campaign finance violation, and which is one of the eight federal crimes that Michael Cohen confessed to and is serving a three-year prison term for?

- what do we give as an explanation for the bungling nature of his staff or political retinue involving such scandals as the spending of hundreds of thousands of dollars on private planes by the former secretary of Health and Human Services Tom Price; the Housing and Urban Development Secretary Ben Carson's indiscretion in allowing his son to help organize an agency listening tour in Baltimore even though he had been warned against it by government lawyers on grounds that it would violate ethics rules?

- how come nothing came out of the claims of sexual assault made by three women against Brett Michael Kavanaugh whom the 45th president of the United States of America nominated to replace Anthony McLeod Kennedy, the 93rd Associate Justice of the

Supreme Court of the United States who served from 1988 until his retirement in 2018 Et cetera?

The above amputations, of course, stand out as a pale shadow of the list of accusations against the 45th president that have proven to be of no consequence. However, that does not mean the president and his retinue are unscathed.

The story of Russian hacking and Russia influencing the 2016 US. presidential election, and the belief that Donald Trump or some members of his team worked with the Russians and other foreign entities to help him win the presidency has clouded the American president's everyday activities for sure. It is as if nothing would assuage the situation for the president; not even the claims by the Russian president Vladimir Putin that there was no Russian involvement in the election, when he stated among other things that *"The hysteria is merely caused by the fact that somebody needs to divert the attention of the American people from the essence of what was exposed by the hackers."*

Many Americans, mostly supporters of Donald Trump think the Russian president is right. They too see a conspiracy by the mainstream media and the Democratic Party to divert attention away from themselves and disarray the Trump presidency and its original intention to cultivate good relations between Russia and the United States of America.

CHAPTER TWO

Verdicts, They Say

"The best gifts to give: To your friend, loyalty; To your enemy, forgiveness; To your boss, service; To a child, a good example; To your parents, gratitude and devotion; To your mate, love and faithfulness; To all men and women, charity."

Oren Arnold

We only have to go back to headline news over the past two and a half dozen months to get a good picture of the damage that the Trump team has suffered as a result of the accusations and charges—both answerable and innocent—heaped by the justice of the land and opponents of the 45th president of the United States of America on him and his team, most of which are centered around the story of Russian interference in the 2016 US Presidential Election and speculations that associates of Donald Trump had links with the Russian nationals who unlawfully intervened in the election. However, it was the supposition that Donald Trump and members of his team colluded with Russia in its alleged interference in the election that sparked off what the Trump camp calls a "Witch Hunt," or what others call a "Russia Hysteria".

To understand the Russia collusion story which was sparked off by the Trump–Russia dossier, otherwise known as the Steele dossier that claims Russia put together a file of compromising information on U.S. President Donald Trump, we have to get to the root of it all. The genesis involves a United States Department of Justice official Bruce G. Ohr and the British national Christopher David Steele who worked as a British intelligence officer with the Secret Intelligence Service MI6 from 1987 until his retirement in 2009. On November 21, 2014, the two men discussed courting Oleg Deripaska, the Russian oligarch noted for his close ties with Russian President Vladimir Putin, to become an asset of the U.S. intelligence. The plan was accelerated in September 2015, three months after Donald Trump formally announced his candidacy at the Trump Tower in New York City, when the FBI and Ohr formally solicited Steele's services to set up a meeting with the Russian billionaire, with the intention to recruit him as an informant on the Kremlin and on organized crime in Russia, in exchange for an American visa. Deripaska would not cooperate and would instead notify the authorities in

Russia about the American effort to recruit him. For that, Bruce Ohr and a number of U.S. government officials decided to revoke Deripaska's US. Visa in 2016.

But then, Fusion GPS, a Washington, D.C-based commercial research and strategic intelligence firm would hire David Steele in June 2016 to research Donald Trump's activities in Russia. Steele's new assignment caused the cooling off of relations with the FBI. However, he would come up with a 35-page document that BuzzFeed News published on January 10, 2017. This controversial material would become known as the Trump–Russia dossier or Steele dossier. It is basically about an extensive Russian conspiracy to elect Trump; and it cited Carter Page, Michael Cohen and other members of Donald Trump's retinue as people who conducted unlawful activities with Russians to realize that objective.

However, those who do not buy the Russia Collusion story see the Steele dossier as a phony. They may have a point after all. On December 21, 2015, Hillary Clinton's campaign chairman John Podesta received an email recommending among other things that their campaign's *"best approach is to slaughter Donald for his bromance with Putin"*. Emails that were stolen from Podesta and the Clinton campaign in the first half of 2016, supposedly by agents of Russia, would be released by WikiLeaks beginning on October 7, 2016. The Clinton camp did not like it, and the vexed Hillary Clinton would blame Russia during the third Clinton-Trump debate on October 19, 2016, for the DNC email leaks and would even accuse

Donald Trump of being a "puppet" of Putin, something Donald Trump denied then and continues to deny today.

As a matter of fact, it wasn't until US. Intelligence learned that George Papadopoulos, a Trump campaign member, had early knowledge of Russians having damaging material on Donald Trump's Democratic Party rival Hillary Clinton that they decided to launch an investigation. The Federal Bureau of Investigation (FBI) reacted by officially opening a covert counterintelligence investigation codenamed "Crossfire Hurricane" on July 31, 2016. Its mission was to find out about links between associates of Donald Trump and Russian officials, and to learn about suspected coordination between Donald Trump's 2016 presidential campaign and the Russian government, especially regarding interference in the 2016 elections in the United States of America.

If Papadopoulos set off the FBI's alarm bells concerning Clinton's emails, Carter Page's spoors set the FBI on his trail. The American Intelligence noted back in January 2015 that a futile attempt was made by a Russian spy ring to recruit Carter Page who at the time was running a one-man investment fund and a consulting company that specialized in oil and gas business in Russia and Central Asia. Carter Page would join Donald Trump's 2016 presidential election campaign in March 2016 and would become Trump's foreign-policy adviser. Following the DNC hacking, and the release of DNC emails by WikiLeaks, the Department of Justice and the FBI would apply for a FISA warrant (a warrant issued by the Foreign Intelligence Surveillance Court—or FISA Court, is actually a tribunal whose actions are carried out in secret—to wiretap a person or persons suspected of spying with or for a foreign government) from the Foreign Intelligence Surveillance Court, to monitor the communications of four officials of the Donald Trump campaign. Instead, on October 21, 2016, they got a warrant to conduct surveillance on and wiretap Carter Page alone, with the approval citing that there is probable cause to believe Page is a Russian agent. That was a month after Carter Page exited the Donald Trump campaign..

In the meantime, on September 19, 2016, Crossfire Hurricane investigators got on the trail of Steele's report. Not long after that, in early October 2016, a team of FBI agents flew to Europe and spoke with Steele about his dossier. There, they learned from Steele that a dossier of allegations compiled by Cody Shearer, a longtime DNC and Clinton operative, fitted *"with what he had separately heard from his own independent sources."* Furthermore, it also involved an unverified allegation that the Russian secret service sexually compromised Donald Trump at the Ritz-Carlton Hotel in Moscow during the American billionaire's visit to Russia in 2013.

From late July to November 2016, through the joint effort by the FBI, the Central Intelligence Agency (CIA), and the National Security Agency (NSA), evidence of Russian meddling in the 2016 United States presidential election was examined. It became apparent during the investigation that the FBI's team enjoyed a large degree of autonomy within the broader interagency probe.

The 2017–2019 Special Counsel investigation took over the FBI's work on May 17, 2017, eventually producing the Mueller Report, which concluded that Russian interference took place in a "sweeping and systematic fashion", that substantial links with the Trump campaign existed, but that the investigators did not get hold of evidence to establish that the Trump campaign "conspired or coordinated" with the government of Russia.

In his book "The Restless Wave." the late Republican Senator John McCain provided intimate details of how he obtained the infamous so-called Steele dossier. He claimed it all started during an annual security conference in Halifax, Nova Scotia, Canada shortly after the November 08, 2016, presidential election, when Sir Andrew Wood, a retired British diplomat told him about it in the presence of Chris Brose, a staff member on the Senate Armed Services Committee, and David Kramer, a former assistant secretary of state with Russian expertise. He wrote thus of Sir Andrew Wood:

> *"He told me he knew a former MI6 officer by the name of Christopher Steele, who had been commissioned to investigate connections between the Trump campaign and Russian agents as well as potentially compromising information about the President-elect that [Russian President Vladimir] Putin allegedly possessed,".*

Senator McCain pointed out that while Sir Andrew Wood thought the information was unverified, the Englishman pointed out that it was information Steele *"strongly believed merited a thorough examination by counterintelligence experts. "*

Under instructions from Senator McCain, Kramer flew to London, met Steele, and then returned with a copy of the report. In his opinion, Steele seemed to be a reputable source. McCain would write that *"The allegations were disturbing, but I had no idea which if any were true..."* Still, on December 9, 2016, the Republican senator whose Vietnam war-hero status was questioned by Donald Trump in July 2015, would hand the report to the director of the FBI, Jim Comey, convinced that he was doing what duty demanded of him.

The fact that Bruce Ohr would lose his position as deputy attorney general in late 2017, while maintaining his position for a time as director of OCDETF; and the fact that he was later demoted by the Department of Justice after the Senate Intelligence Committee found out about his meetings with Christopher Steele and Glenn Simpson, the founder of Fusion GPS, explain why many people, especially supporters of Donald Trump, think it was Steele's bias against Trump that resulted in the Special Counsel investigation and the media buzz that distracted the Trump administration from carrying out its duties in a more effective manner.

In a nutshell, the Federal Bureau of Investigation (FBI) covertly started investigations into the activities of Russian operatives and members of the Trump presidential campaign back in July 2016. However, it was not until after Donald trump's inauguration in January 2017 that these investigations expanded from, among other things, a probe into the interaction between Russia and the Trump transition team and the release of emails during the presidential campaign by WikiLeaks, into what became a full-blown investigation of some members of the President's team. Otherwise called the Special Counsel Investigation or Mueller Investigation, the probe ran from May 2017 to March 2019, a period and its aftermath that some Trump supporters view as a lost period of his presidency. The American lawyer and university administrator Jerry Falwell Jr., who is serving as the president of Liberty University in Lynchburg, Virginia, expressed his indignation on what he considered the distracting influence of the Mueller Investigation with the following words:

"I now support reparations—Trump should have 2 yrs added to his 1st term as payback for time stolen by this corrupt failed coup…"

Jerry Falwell Jr., Donald Trump, past and current members of the president's team, Trump supporters and the wide range of Americans and foreigners who take an interest in American politics have every reason to raise their eyebrows because not only did the Mueller investigation absolve Donald Trump and his retinue of the much-talked-about charge of Collusion with Russia, it failed to clear the air on Russian "Interference" in the classic sense of the word when it comes to influencing the outcome of an election as most people know it or as it is considered unacceptable in international relations. So the fact that the Democratic Party and the left-wing media continues taking in an incessant manner about the Special Counsel investigation; the fact that the anti-Trump forces in the country and abroad continue to dwell on speculations that the president obstructed justice or tried to influence the investigation and so should be impeached, hardens the resolve of Trump's core supporters and those who are sympathetic towards the colorful former media mogul or are inclined to be tenderhearted towards the beleaguered president. And these are people who in the first place, saw the whole investigation as a conspiracy.

On May 17.2019, a twist developed in the story of collusion with Russia, which during and right after the Mueller investigation had morphed into "Obstruction of Justice", when the report showed that there was no collusion between the Trump campaign and the Russians to secure a victory for Donald Trump in the 2016 presidential election. Supporters of the troubled president consider "Obstruction of Justice" as nothing but another baseless outlet or argument brought up by his opponents as perhaps their last resort to prevent the maverick from serving his full term in office or from winning a second term in the upcoming 2020 presidential election.

A person interested in the political intrigues or conspiracies taking place in Washington DC does not have to focus only on members of the Democratic Party to find politicians who among other things think the president's character flaws make him intolerably unpresidential. The Republican Party that pundits thought had rallied behind the president, especially after the death of the former Republican Senator John McCain, experienced a chink in its armor when Justin Amash, a Republican Congressman from Michigan, thrust himself into the limelight by breaking with his Republican colleagues through claims made in public that the Mueller Report had *"...multiple examples of conduct satisfying all the elements of obstruction of justice, and undoubtedly any person who is not the president of the United States would be indicted based on such evidence"*. This happened despite the fact that the US. attorney general William Barr had told Congress just weeks before that based on Mueller's report and the summary he made from it in March 2019, Donald Trump did not obstruct justice during the investigation.

While the attorney general's conclusion certainly went a long way towards exonerating Donald Trump and energizing his supporters, it disheartened a large faction of Trump opponents who immediately concluded that William Barr was siding with the president and as such should not be trusted. It became apparent afterward that William Barr's May 01, 2019 appearance at the Senate Judiciary Committee and the testimony he gave on Robert S. Mueller III's report, still failed to convince most of Donald Trump's opponents to change their positions. So, only a holy fool, who is clueless about the intrigues of politics, would have been surprised when those seeking Donald Trump's scalp called on Robert Mueller to make a public statement or testify in person about the matter.

That is why when Amash went further by adding that: *"Contrary to Barr's portrayal...Mueller's report reveals that President Trump engaged in specific actions and a pattern of behavior that meet the threshold for impeachment...",* he practically threw the gauntlet down on the Republican Party that he is a member of and made it inevitable for Robert Mueller to say something.

Amash's call for an impeachment of Donald Trump over allegations, which so far are unproven, that he obstructed justice has sparked off claims by people, most of whom are on the side of the president, that he is a libertarian posing as a Republican. As a matter of fact, Amash heads the House Liberty Caucus, which is generally regarded as a "conservative group with a libertarian emphasis", and which is associated with the Tea Party movement. The members of the House Liberty Caucus are Republicans of the United States House of Representatives that ideologically are either conservatives, libertarians, or libertarian conservatives. The group's libertarian-minded philosophy is rooted in the conviction that the only way the GOP can win more elections in the future is for the Republican Party to accept their libertarian-minded philosophy because voters are embracing it, especially after the recent government data collection revelations that many voters believe infringes on their rights to privacy.

Justin Amash's submission of his resignation to Republican Leader Kevin McCarthy and House Republican Conference Leader Liz Cheney on July 8, 2019, barely days after making public his intention to leave the Republican Party, still came as a surprise to many.

Not cowed by challenges from the opposition and Amash, the special prosecutor or head of the Special investigation publicly spoke about the investigation on May 29, 2019, pointing out in particular that:

- the United States of America was under "concerted attack" by a foreign power during the 2016 elections
- there was no criminal conspiracy or "collusion" between the "Russians" who carried out the cyber-attacks and members of the Trump campaign team
- and that *"There was insufficient evidence to charge a broader conspiracy,"* and that *"Charging the president with a crime was therefore not an option…"* they could consider.

Donald Trump's noteworthy reply to Mueller's statement was a tweet that read thus:

"Nothing changes from the Mueller Report. There was insufficient evidence and therefore, in our country, a person is innocent. The case is closed! Thank you."

Hard as they tried, the Trump team failed to come across as people with a firm conviction that Robert Mueller spoke in their favor in his public statement that also told Americans he was retiring as special counsel and that the office would be shut down. However, Democrats and other opponents of Donald Trump found enough ammunition in Mueller's words to use against the president, especially the sentence by the special counsel that *"There was insufficient evidence to charge a broader conspiracy...",* and a point he made that the report never said the president was innocent. Even though Mueller also said that *"...I hope and expect this to be the only time that I will speak about this matter,"* Democrats in Congress demanded his appearance before their committees to answer questions, hoping that he would provide more ammunition that would buttress their case for an impeachment of the president.

That is why he publicly testified on July 24, 2019, in the House of Representatives about his investigation into Russian interference in the 2016 election. It was a double-header —an 8:30 a.m. testimony at the House Judiciary Committee, and another at noon at the House Intelligence Committee. Mueller's testimony brought nothing new to the table and actually exonerated Donald Trump far more than William Barr's testimony on and summary of the Mueller report did.

Regardless of how Donald Trump and his supporters try to interpret it, the Amash hiccup in the Republican Party is an extension of the setbacks the Trump team has suffered over the past two years, misfortunes per se that can be attributed to the Special Counsel Investigation. Amash's call for an impeachment, irrespective of how naïve some would say it sounds, is anchored on the grounds that some people who were a part of either the Trump campaign team or the Trump administration, or both, have been found guilty of crimes that were not what the Special Counsel Investigation was created to investigate, leaving many wondering whether the whole investigation was not a witch-hunt after all. To judge for ourselves, we only have to take a look at some of the victims or culprits of the Mueller investigation who not only got fined but served or are serving terms in jail.

I: Paul John Manafort Jr.

Many pundits consider the renowned American lawyer, lobbyist and political consultant Paul John Manafort Jr. as the biggest of the fishes that the Special Counsel investigation netted. Though first arrested by the FBI on October 30, 2017, after an indictment by a federal grand jury as part of Robert Mueller's investigation into the Trump campaign, Paul Manafort ended up facing unrelated charges to the story of Collusion with Russia, so that the Eastern District of Virginia court winded up convicting him on August 21, 2018, on five counts of tax fraud, two counts of bank fraud, and on failure to disclose his foreign bank accounts. The court sentenced him to 47 months in jail. This was followed by another conviction on March 13, 2019, from the District Court for the District of Columbia, giving him 43 months in jail, 30 of which he would have to serve concurrently with jail time he received from the Eastern District of Virginia. In this second case, a conspiracy to defraud the United States of America accounted for 30 of the 43 months, and witness tampering accounted for the remaining 13 months. Manafort actually thought he could avoid a second sentencing by making a plea deal with prosecutors and by pleading guilty to the two charges on September 14, 2018. However, a court filing by

Mueller's office on November 26, 2018, holding Manafort responsible for breaching the plea deal was supported by the DC District Court Judge Amy Berman Jackson, who ruled on February 13, 2019, that he violated his plea deal by lying repeatedly to prosecutors. As things stand now, Manafort is expected to be released from the Federal Correctional Institution in Loretto, Pennsylvania on December 25, 2024.

As if in a bid to forestall a presidential pardon, prosecutors in the state of New York charged Manafort with residential mortgage fraud, conspiracy and the falsification of business records. The action, which happened barely minutes after the March 13, 2019, second sentencing hearing, put him at risk of additional prison time if found guilty. The law of the land—New York—states that a presidential pardon cannot override or influence a sentence if he gets convicted. Paul Manafort and his defense team see double jeopardy in the New York state case, and so acted accordingly during his summon to the New York state's Supreme Court on June 27, 2019—his third criminal case in recent years—by pleading not guilty to state fraud charges brought against him by the office of the Manhattan district attorney.

Contrary to expectations, Manafort's case could have been a witch-hunt after all. Even so, it could only be one that was not initially targeted at Donald Trump. In a way, the president-to-be at the time just found himself on Manafort's trial that March 2016, the day the aesthetic-political consultant joined Donald Trump's presidential campaign team. Manafort's sympathizers claim that among his many "crimes", the gravest was the consulting work he did in Ukraine for the government of Ukraine's fourth president Viktor Yanukovych, the Russia-leaning native of the country's premier industrial city and region of Donetsk, before the pro-Russian Yanukovych was overthrown on February 22, 2014 by an American/European Union-backed uprising called EuroMaidan, on grounds that he suspended the signing of an association agreement between Ukraine and the European Union, and that he chose closer ties to Russia and the Russian-led Eurasian Economic Union instead. Only after that forceful change of power in Ukraine did the FBI reportedly begin an investigation of Paul Manafort in 2014, the same year that Russia is reported to have started its anti-US campaign, which was well before Donald Trump began his campaign to become the 45th president of the United States of America. In fact, when Donald Trump tweeted that, *"Russia started their anti-US campaign in 2014, long before I announced that I would run for President...The results of the election were not impacted. The Trump campaign did nothing wrong—no collusion!"* we see that his reasoning was backed by logic.

However, it wasn't until the eve of Donald Trump's inauguration that the public first learned of the activities of multiple federal agencies investigating Paul Manafort, prominent among which were the Central Intelligence Agency (CIA), Federal Bureau of Investigation (FBI), the Director of National Intelligence (DNI), the National Security Agency (NSA), and the financial crimes unit of the Treasury Department. As a matter of fact, the American political establishment regarded Yanukovych as a pro-

Russian candidate back in 2004 when he ran against the pro-American candidate Viktor Yushchenko in the run-off vote of the Ukrainian presidential election of November 21, 2004, which in the opinion of several domestic and foreign election monitors, was rigged by the authorities in favor of Yanukovych, an electoral fraud per se that sparked off protests that compelled the country's Supreme Court to annul the results of the run-off and order a revote for December 26, 2004. Viktor Yushchenko emerged victorious from that rerun by clinching 52% of the votes. So, the fact that Manafort helped bring Yanukovych back to power on March 22, 2006 while serving as a political consultant whose team effectively managed and directed the campaign of Yanukovych's political party —Party of the Regions —to the point where the pro-Russian party won the 2006 Ukrainian parliamentary election with 32% of the votes, whence Yanukovych became the Prime Minister of Ukraine from August 04, 2006 – December 18, 2007, ruffled feathers in Washington DC and the capitals of several European countries. These were people who saw the upsetting Yanukovych victory as an unexpected setback in their plans for Ukraine, a setback caused by an American private citizen for that matter.

Many of the decision-makers in the Washington bureaucracy and the American political establishment, in general, did not find it funny at all that Paul Manafort continued working with Yanukovych and his Party of the Regions, and that he played a prominent role in making the Donetsk native win the run-off vote of the 2010 Ukrainian presidential election against the US/EU-backed Yulia

Tymoshenko. To add further insult to injury, Yulia Tymoshenko was sentenced to seven years in jail on October 11, 2011, for allegedly abusing her office as Prime Minister of Ukraine when brokering the gas deal Ukraine signed with Russia in 2009. Her supporters in the West called her incarceration a witch hunt. She was only released after the overthrow of her nemesis Viktor Yanukovych.

The 2010 setback in the game plan of the Western powers over Ukraine automatically made the American political consultant an enemy of the forces in the United States of America and the European Union that had been working for decades to pull Ukraine away from Russia and into the orbit of the European Union and NATO. Per Victoria Nuland, who served in the US. State Department from September 18, 2013 – January 25, 2017, as the Assistant Secretary of State for European and Eurasian Affairs, the EuroMaidan was planned and sponsored at the cost of $5 billion. Ukraine got subverted all right; Yanukovych got ousted from power, but at a huge cost. Russia annexed the much-coveted Crimea Peninsular that Ukraine received from Russia in 1956 when both countries were constituent republics of the USSR (Union of Soviet Socialist Republics); Yanukovych's stronghold of Donbass (constituting the provinces of Donetsk and Lugansk) rebelled against the new authorities in Kiev, sparking off a civil war that has seen Ukraine lose a further ten percent of its population and a quarter of its industrial heartland, so that the world is now left with the dilemma of how to deal with two unrecognized republics called Donetsk People's Republic (DNR) and Lugansk People's Republic (LNR), both of which are abashedly pro-Russian.

Today, Ukraine is in a geopolitical limbo as it appears the enthusiasm of the European Union and the USA for the country has mellowed. The new political leadership under the anti-Russian oligarch Petro Poroshenko that the EuroMaidan brought to power got discredited as corruption worsened during the five years that they held power, as the economic situation of the country failed to improve, as the authorities failed to rein in the extreme right, and as Ukraine lost more than a quarter of its population through emigration, the loss of Crimea, and the war in the Donbass. Ukrainians voters expressed their disappointment with the first post EuroMaidan leadership by voting Poroshenko out of office in the run-off vote of the 21 April 2019 Ukrainian presidential election where he garnered 24.45% of the votes against the 73.22% won by his opponent Volodymyr Zelensky, a comedian, actor and screenwriter who before the election had held no political office, had never contested an election and basically had no political experience.

II: Michael Cohen

Though not as big in stature as Paul Manafort, Michael Dean Cohen, the man who played the role of Donald Trump's personal lawyer from 2007-2018, is perhaps the most colorful and sensational of the close Trump associates who got charged and convicted following an inquisition by the Special Counsel investigation on his activities prior to and after the 2016 presidential election. He was sentenced to three years in prison on December 12, 2018, for federal income taxes evasion, for his involvement in the payment of hush money to two women on behalf of Donald Trump before the 2016 presidential election and for making false statements to banks and the United States Congress. As a matter of fact, he even pleaded guilty to the nine felony charges that got him convicted and he agreed to cooperate with investigators looking not only into Russian interference in the election but into the Trump Organization's business practices as well.

When Michael Cohen told the court at his sentencing that *"It was my duty to cover up his dirty deeds,"* he widened the phase of conflict with his former boss because Donald Trump countered that Michael Cohen, whom the media sensationally referred to as Donald Trump's "fixer" before his investigation that led him to plead guilty on August 21, 2018, was lying. All the same, when the U.S. District Judge William H. Pauley III sentenced Cohen to three years in prison, fined him $50,000 fine, ordered him to pay $1.4 million in restitution and made him forfeit $500,000, he certainly dealt a heavy blow to the president's former personal lawyer.

How did it get to that point where Donald Trump's personal lawyer of more than a decade would work against him, to the point of even calling Donald Trump a "racist," a "con man", and a "cheat" during a public televised testimony before the House Oversight Committee that lasted 10 hours?

Things started falling apart on April 9, 2018, when acting on an federal warrant based on a referral by the Special Counsel investigation, the FBI raided Michael Cohen's law office, his home, and his hotel room, carrying away implicating documents and records, with payments made to Stormy Daniels by Michael Cohen featuring among the documentation. And this was just a month after Stormy Daniels (born Stephanie Gregory) actually came to command the political and media limelight due to her March 25, 2018, interview with *60 Minutes* where she talked of having a onetime sexual affair with Donald Trump back in 2006, and as a result was later threatened in front of her infant daughter to keep quiet about the liaison, compelling her to take $130,000 in hush money, and to sign a non-disclosure agreement in October 2016, shortly before the presidential election.

As a matter of fact, the gossip magazine *Life & Style* and the blog *The Dirty* had actually published the story of the alleged affair back in 2011, and Michael Cohen had stopped another gossip magazine called *In Touch Weekly* from publishing the story by threatening to sue it. So when *The Wall Street Journal* reported the story on January 12, 2018, and mentioned that Michael Cohen paid Stormy Daniels $130,000, one month before the presidential election, the international daily newspaper compelled the Trump lawyer to respond. On February 13, 2018, Michael Cohen gave some credence to the story and probably triggered the hunt that got him incarcerated when he released a carefully worded statement to the New York

Times, part of which read thus:

> *"In a private transaction in 2016, I used my own personal funds to facilitate a payment of $130,000 to Ms. Stephanie Clifford...Neither the Trump Organization nor the Trump campaign was a party to the transaction with Ms. Clifford, and neither reimbursed me for the payment, either directly or indirectly."*

The fact that on April 30, 2018, a day after the raid on Cohen's abodes, Stormy Daniels filed a lawsuit against Donald Trump on libel charges because the president called her statements and a previous lawsuit a "fraud", tells a lot about the way the belligerents timed their actions. She had actually filed her March 6, 2018 lawsuit against Donald Trump on the grounds that the non-disclosure agreement she signed was invalid because Donald Trump never personally signed it. However, it wasn't until Michael Cohen pleaded guilty on August 21, 2018, to violating finance laws during the 2016 presidential election by handling hush money for Mr. Trump's alleged lovers that the public became aware of a rift between him and the Donald Trump. That was when his personal lawyer, Lanny Davis said Michael Cohen was prepared to *"tell everything about Donald Trump that he knows"*. This apparent conversion from Trump's personal lawyer or "fixer" to Trump's potential "nemesis" seemed to have gone a nudge up when Cohen re-registered as a Democrat on October 11, 2018, nineteen months after abandoning his membership in the party by registering as a Republican back on March 9, 2017.

Donald Trump's former lawyer would live up to the promise to be forthcoming about his past working relationship with Donald Trump when he pleaded guilty on November 29, 2018 to a charge brought up by the Special Counsel investigation that he lied to the Senate Intelligence Committee and House Intelligence Committee in 2017 about the 2015 and 2016 proposed Trump Tower Moscow deal that he spearheaded. The reason he gave for that act of perjury was that he wanted his statements to be in line with Donald Trump's *"repeated disavowals of commercial and political ties between himself and Russia"*. Despite receiving a two-month sentence, to be served concurrently with his three-year sentence, he apparently did not regress in his change of heart when he appeared before the House Oversight Committee on February 27, 2019, expressed remorse and shame for some of the things he did as Donald Trump's personal lawyer, and then went as far as pointing out that the president reimbursed him for the illegal hush payments he made.

It appears Michael Cohen's February 28, 2019, and his March 6, 2019, closed doors testimonies to the House Intelligence Committee provided some more information about the president that some elected officials, especially of the Democratic Party, think they can use to bring the Trump presidency to a premature end. If that is truly the case, then the American public and those abroad who find the Trump collusion saga worth their attention, should be expecting another twist in the tale with Michael Cohen serving as a major catalyst. And coming from a man who once claimed he would take a bullet for Donald Trump, such a stand would be an intriguing development indeed.

III: George Papadopoulos

Another person who also found himself in the crosshairs of the Special Counsel investigation was George Papadopoulos, a polyglot per se who speaks Arabic, English, French, and Greek. In what is considered a plea bargain reflecting his cooperation with the Mueller investigation, the former foreign policy adviser in Donald Trump's campaign team pleaded guilty on October 05, 2017 to lying to FBI agents about contacts he had with a possible agent working for Russian interest who claimed to have "dirt" on Hillary Clinton. He was sentenced to 14 days in jail on Sept. 7, 2018, to December 7, 2018, but is currently under a 12-month supervised release.

In his book entitled *"Deep State Target: How I Got Caught in the Crosshairs of the Plot to Bring Down President Trump"*, George Papadopoulos gives his side of the story and his analysis of the whole affair, surmising that he and several Trump campaign associates were entrapped by the Special Counsel investigation and some of the country's security services.

So, how did the young smart-eyed energy consultant who at the age of twenty-eight worked for Ben Carson's campaign from December 2015 to February 2016, then went on to join the Trump campaign a month later, become entangled in such a major case involving international conspiracies that he claimed to be unaware of at the time?

The answer lies in Papadopoulos's role in the Trump campaign as the man who set up meetings with foreign leaders, a role that put him in regular contact with high-ranking campaign officials. His go-between responsibility inadvertently exposed him to insidious characters of which the most prominent turned out to be a Maltese academic called Joseph Mifsud. According to what some prominent figures in the investigation said, Mifsud had high-level connections to the Russian government. So the fact that Papadopoulos met him twice and was told on the second occasion that Russia had "dirt" on Hillary Clinton, raised suspicions that could not be easily dismissed. However, what made him a possible target for America's security apparatus was his May 10, 2016, meeting with top Australian diplomat Alexander John Gosse Downer in London where he allegedly told the Aussie about the "dirt" on Hillary Clinton, who at the time was under scrutiny for deleting thousands of her emails. Downer would inform the FBI about it and the FBI would open a counterintelligence investigation on George Papadopoulos and other associates of Donald Trump in connection with attempts by Russia to disrupt the 2016 US. presidential election. That was following the hacking, by alleged Russian intelligence agents, of the Democratic National Committee where emails were stolen by one or more hackers who were operating under the pseudonym "Guccifer 2.0", and of the emails of John Podesta, the chairman of the 2016 Hillary Clinton presidential campaign; and this was after the hacked information got leaked or published by DC Leaks in June and July 2016, and by WikiLeaks on July 22, 2016.

Though Papadopoulos rued not reporting Mifsud's comment about "dirt" on Hillary Clinton to the US. Intelligence right away, and though he accepted that he was in favor of better cooperation with Russia, he denied making any outreach to the Russian government. However, FBI agents would interview him on January 27, 2017, regarding Trump campaign links with Russia. This would be followed by his arrest without a warrant on July 27, 2017, soon after he landed at the Washington-Dulles International Airport from a flight from abroad. And that too was a few days after he received $10,000 as a retainer from a man in Israel he claimed gave him the creeps, but who declared the purpose of the money as his intention to do business with Papadopoulos.

So when on May 14, 2019, George Papadopoulos told Maria Bartiromo of Fox Business News that investigators should examine the $10,000 cash payment he received from the man he alleges was a spy, he seemed to be siding with Donald Trump on his Spygate conspiracy theory that the administration of his predecessor Barack Obama implanted a spy in his 2016 presidential campaign for political purposes. Papadopoulos all the same raised more questions than provided answers in this excerpt of his interview:

"...I get to Dulles, I have FBI agents scrambling, they don't even know why they're arresting me, I have no arrest warrant waiting for me, I'm not told why I am being arrested. And later I find out from a report that came out a couple of days ago that Andrew Weissmann and Mueller's team was in touch with officials in Cyprus, I think the legal attaché over there, to discuss Paul Manafort and myself, because I was actually in Cyprus over that summer.

So something the insidious was going on here. I think these bills that are still in Athens right now must be examined by the investigators, because I think they are marked and they're going to go all the way back to DOJ, under the previous FBI under Comey, and even the Mueller team.

If the Mueller team is going around entrapping campaign associates and Trump associates, the way they did to me, I am sure it wasn't just me they did it to, and it is going to open up a massive can of worms and I think we need to get to the bottom of exactly, not only how did this story start, but why were they entrapping us moving forward..."

Convinced that the bills of the $10,000 he received were marked, George Papadopoulos went further during the interview and demanded that the banknotes be reviewed by Congress, William Barr, the Inspector General of the

United States Department of Justice Michael E. Horowitz, as well as John W. Huber who was appointed by U.S. Attorney General Jeff Sessions in 2017 to start investigation on the FBI's surveillance of Carter Page and on connections between the Clinton Foundation and Uranium One. George Papadopoulos also requested the input of other agencies and investigators.

Some pundits consider the Papadopoulos affair hazy for multiple reasons, citing as examples from an array of indications, Downer's 28 April 2018 interview with *The Australian*—Australia's most circulated nationally distributed newspaper—where he said among other things that *"...nothing [Papadopoulos] said in their meeting indicated Trump himself had been conspiring with the Russians to collect information on Hillary Clinton.";* as well as the fact that Joseph Mifsud *"is missing and may be deceased"*, a piece of information from the September 2018 filing in a U.S. federal court in the case *Democratic National Committee v. Russian Federation* that certainly raises eyebrows.

IV: Alex Van Der Zwaan

The Belgian-born Dutchman Alex van der Zwaan was the first person sentenced to prison in connection with the Special Counsel investigation on possible collusion with Russia. However, the attorney's 30-day sentence was grounded on the fact that he pleaded guilty to lying to federal agents about his contacts in September 2016 with the deputy chair of Donald Trump's campaign Rick Gates, while answering questions about Russian interference in the 2016 elections in the USA.

It was, however, Alex van der Zwaan's working relationship with Paul Manafort that set him on the radar of the FBI, the CIA, and the United States of America's other security apparatus. His time working as an attorney in the London office of the international law firm Skadden, Arps, Slate, Meagher & Flom LLP from 2007-2017, saw him doing several consulting works on Russia and Ukraine for his company. It was also during this time that he found his wife—the daughter of the Ukrainian-born German Borisovich Khan, a wealthy co-owner of Russia's Alfa Bank who besides standing out as a holder of Ukrainian, Russian, and Israeli citizenships, has his name mentioned in the infamous dossier written by the former British intelligence officer Christopher Steele, in essence a controversial account that triggered the Russia Collusion story. In fact, German Khan and his fellow Alfa Bank owners Mikhail Fridman and Petr Aven, filed a defamation lawsuit against BuzzFeed in May 2017, accusing the American Internet media, news and entertainment company of publishing the unverified Trump–Russia dossier that alleged financial ties and collusion between Donald Trump, the Russian President Vladimir Putin and the three owners of Alfa Bank.

Alex van der Zwaan's connection to Manafort and Rick Gates sprouted from the 2012 report that the government of the then Ukrainian president Viktor Yanukovych commissioned Skadden Arps to work on, via Manafort—a nasty piece of work, per the then United States ambassador to Ukraine John E. Herbst, against Ukraine's pro-western former prime minister Yulia Tymoshenko that was effectively used to defend her 2011 prosecution, conviction and seven-year imprisonment that was only shortened by the 2014 Euromaidan. Alex van der Zwaan was however arraigned for his dissemination of an unfavorable report on Yulia Tymoshenko in the USA and other Western countries, and for allegedly lying about his 2016 communications with Rick Gates and Manafort's longtime business associate Konstantin Kilimnik, whom the special counsel considered a former Russia intelligence officer.

The fact that in January 2019, Skadden Arps agreed to pay the sum of $4.6 million as settlement to the Department of Justice for its investigation into the work the firm did with Paul Manafort and for the retroactive filing of proper foreign lobbying paperwork, tells us a lot about the Ukrainian connection in Alex van der Zwaan's fall from grace. And the fact that he got deported after serving his prison term goes to explain the outsized role the Ukraine connection played in the whole collusion story in the eyes of some people.

V: Richard Pinedo

A case that did not receive much attention by the mainstream media was the October 10, 2018 sentencing by the United States District Judge Dabney L. Friedrich of the computer whiz Richard Pinedo to six months in jail and six months of home confinement for identity fraud owing to

his role in running an online server company called
Auction Essistance which was involved in the buying and
selling of bank account numbers that helped the users
circumvent the security measures of digital payment
companies such as eBay and PayPal. An illegal action per
se, Richard Pinedo had the extra misfortune of selling these
fake online identities to 13 Russians who used them to buy
ads on Facebook. These Russians got indicted by the
Special Counsel investigation for interfering in the 2016
presidential election.

Auction Essistance's core business, which involved
brokering bank account numbers, made it possible for
people who had been barred from websites such as PayPal
and eBay, to do business with those websites again, but
under a different identity. Actually, Richard Pinedo ran the
line for two years until he caught the eye of the country's
security agencies and the Mueller team. In his February 2,
2018 plea agreement, the young man pleaded guilty to two
felony charges of identity fraud, and of using the identity of
other individuals for "unlawful activity". By cooperating
fully with the investigation, the fifteen years in federal
prison and a fine of $250,000 that such a crime carries with
it as punishment got scaled down to the limited jail
sentence he got, so that he is a free man today. In fact,
when he told the court on the day of his sentencing that,

> *"I take full responsibility for what I've done...I've
> tried to do everything possible to help in this
> investigation,"*

he made himself one of the most cooperative indictees that the Special Counsel Investigation worked with.

CHAPTER THREE

Collusion and Limbo

"If you want to make peace with your enemy, you have to work with your enemy. Then he becomes your partner."

Nelson Mandela

"If you tell the truth, you don't have to remember anything."

Mark Twain

"Whoever would overthrow the liberty of a nation must begin by subduing the freeness of speech."

Benjamin Franklin

There is a sense of ambivalence when it comes to the nature of the cases involving some of the individuals pinned down by the Special Counsel investigation. The nature of their exculpations, pending verdicts and cooperation leaves the ground fertile for all sorts of conspiracy theories to develop. We only have to look into some of these cases to draw our own conclusions.

I: Michael Thomas Flynn

The second big fish in the Trump camp that got netted by the Special Counsel Investigation was Donald Trump's first national security adviser Michael Thomas Flynn, who served in the Trump administration from January 23, 2017 – February 13, 2017. His longest career was with the United States Army where he served for 33 years until he retired on August 2014 with the rank of Lieutenant-General. He went into business right after his time with the US. Army.

Michael Flynn is considered by some to be an even bigger fish than Paul Manafort. He was compelled to resign from the Trump administration on February 13, 2017, only after he became privy to information that he had misled the FBI and the US. Vice President Mike Pence about the nature and content of his communications with Sergey Kislyak, who at the time was the Russian Ambassador to the United States of America.

After several close investigations and close engagements with different federal agencies, Michael Flynn pleaded guilty on December 1, 2017 to "willfully and knowingly" making "false, fictitious and fraudulent statements" to the FBI about a $530,000 consulting contract he had with the Dutch company Inovo BV, which was primarily intended to benefit Turkey's government, and about his conversations with Sergey Kislyak, even though he specified later that during his December 29, 2016 conversation with the Russian ambassador, he asked the foreign diplomat *"to refrain from escalating...in response to sanctions that the United States had imposed against Russia that same day."* Michael Flynn has so far not been sentenced, even though several attempts at doing so ended up in deferrals. In fact, the Mueller investigation suggested that he should receive little or no time in jail, a point confirmed by a sentencing memorandum that was released on December 4, 2018, stating that Michael Flynn *"deserves credit for accepting responsibility in a timely fashion and substantially assisting the government".*

However, it was Michael Flynn's association with businesses and governments that led to complaints about possible conflicts of interest and one criminal charge levied against him. It is widely claimed that the impressive number and substance of business ventures that he amassed after his retirement from the military to the time he became Donald Trump's national security adviser on January 23, 2017, was his undoing. During that period in business, he served on the board of several organizations, while also running a consulting firm that provided intelligence services for businesses and governments. Flynn Intel Group Inc, as the consulting firm was called, evolved with time to include subsidiaries.

Just like Paul Manafort, Flynn too was in the cross-hairs of several federal agencies before he got incorporated into the Trump team. In fact, shortly after the 2016 presidential election, he even made it known to the transition team counsel Don McGahn that he was under federal investigation for secretly lobbying for Turkey during the campaign. President Obama's warning back on November 10, 2018, to President-elect Donald Trump against hiring Michael Flynn, as well as Chris Christie's counseling to Trump against making the retired Lieutenant General his national security adviser, all go to explain the extent of the beef the Obama administration and the intelligence agencies were having with Michael Flynn. Curiously enough, it was President Barack Obama who appointed Michael Flynn as the 18th Director of the Defense Intelligence Agency, a post he served from July 24, 2012 – August 7, 2014.

Even before his apparent forced retirement after 33 years in service, Michael Flynn had expressed his doubts about the Obama administration's narrative that Al-Qaeda was on the verge of defeat. He had also questioned the wisdom in toppling the Syrian strongman Bashar Al-Assad, basing his arguments on the grounds that the Syrian insurgency was dominated by radical Islamists who were dedicated to creating an Islamic Caliphate. By taking such a stand, Michael Flynn automatically made himself an implacable opponent of those in the Obama administration, the bureaucracy the political establishment, and even some influential foreign allies. Besides, the former military man, among other things, continued criticizing Obama's Middle Eastern policy during the presidential campaign, to the point of:

- even stating on July 11, 2016, that he was a "pro-life Democrat"
- calling on the United States to "work constructively with Russia" in Syria
- opposing the Iran nuclear deal
- lobbying for the government of Turkish President Recep Tayyip Erdoğan even after the July 15, 2016 attempted coup d'état against the Turkish strongman that Erdoğan responded to with a purge and a call on the United States of America to "...extradite Fethullah Gülen" to Turkey, even though he knew the Turkish Islamic scholar, political leader, and preacher was his arch-rival. As a matter of fact, the Turkish president's actions and policies started distancing Turkey slowly from its western allies years ago.
- above all, opening the way for the staunch Democrats in the intelligence and security apparatus to view him as a turncoat, especially after he joined the Trump team.

II: Rick Gates

A case in the Special Counsel investigation whose outcome is highly anticipated is that of Rick Gates, the former business partner of Paul Manafort who is better known as Donald Trump's ex-campaign chairman serving time in prison. Rick Gates worked for Manafort before and during the campaign. The Gates and Manafort tandem did not only involve Gates working with Manafort on a couple of deals, one of which is the consulting job they did for the deposed Ukrainian president Viktor Yanukovych. In fact, Rick James at one point was the deputy chairman of Donald Trump's presidential campaign and even headed Trump's inaugural committee. The fact that he pleaded guilty in February 2018 to lying to FBI agents and to a conspiracy against the United States of America as a result of his work with Paul Manafort for the benefit of the former Ukrainian president while operating as an unregistered lobbyist, leaves much room for speculation.

The Virginian born and based Rick Gates first crossed paths with Paul Manafort during his internship at the consulting firm called Black, Manafort, Stone, and Kelly. He impressed on the Republican lobbyist Rick Davis while working at the firm's Washington, D.C office. That was why after Rick Davis and Paul Manafort formed a new consulting firm in 2006 called Davis Manafort, he thought Rick Gates could be relied upon, and so hired him. With an office in the Ukrainian capital city of Kyiv, Davis Manafort would solicit clients in the Eastern Slavic world, eventually working for the Ukrainian politician and later Ukrainian president Viktor Yanukovych, as well as other clients such as the Russian oligarch Oleg Deripaska who among other things, owned one of the largest diversified industrial groups in Russia called Basic Element Ltd. Gates became invaluable to the consulting company to the point where he played a major role in brokering a meeting in 2006 between the then-senator and presidential hopeful John McCain and the Russian oligarch Deripaska. So it came as no surprise that after Rick Davis left Davis Manafort in 2008 and joined John McCain's presidential campaign team, Rick James became his logical replacement in the firm. That was how his fortunes or misfortunes rose in the company to the point where he was next to Paul Manafort in the foreign consulting work that helped Yanukovych and his party win the 2006 parliamentary election and the 2010 presidential election that marked Yanukovych's political comeback and domination of Ukrainian politics respectively; that is, until his overthrow in 2014.

It is difficult to find anyone who would say that Rick Gates's career and life did not take the turn into the abyss when he started working for the Trump campaign in June 2016 after Donald Trump made Paul Manafort his campaign manager. Manafort did not hesitate to promote him to the post of deputy campaign manager in charge of handling the campaign's day-to-day activities as if he could not be effective in the top campaign job without his subordinate of ten years.

Rick Gates would prove to be invaluable indeed because Donald Trump would go on to win the 2016 presidential election. However, when a federal grand jury indicted Rick Gates and Paul Manafort on October 27, 2017, as part of the investigation into Russian interference in the 2016

United States elections as well as related matters that the Special Counsel investigation was conducting, it was found that there was more to the Rick Gates story than met the eye. However, he and Manafort would plead not guilty at their October 30, 2017 court hearing to the twelve-count indictment charging them with conspiracy against the United States of America, with making false statements, with money laundering, and with failing to register as foreign agents for Ukraine as required by the Foreign Agents Registration Act.

Things took an unexpected turn when Robert Mueller revealed new charges in the Manafort and Gates case on February 22, 2018, thereby bringing the counts to 32— sixteen counts of false individual income tax returns, seven counts related to failure to file reports of financial and foreign bank accounts, five counts of bank fraud conspiracy, and four counts of bank fraud. Rick Gates responded to the development by pleading guilty on February 23, 2018, to one count of conspiracy against the United States of America and one count of making false statements. He also agreed to cooperate with the Mueller investigation. He would later work as a star witness against Paul Manafort, providing the Special Counsel investigation with an insight into the extensive seven-year criminal conspiracy he engaged with Manafort ranging from lying to the Internal Revenue Service, to money-laundering, to inflating his expense accounts with phony charges, to avoiding the payment of taxes, and to falsifying documents to banks in order to obtain millions of dollars in loans.

III Roger Stone

Roger Stone, a colorful political consultant and longtime associate of Donald Trump happens to be one of the popular names arraigned in connection with the Special Counsel investigation but that no judgment has yet been passed on. As only an informal adviser to the Trump campaign, he logically was not supposed to feature in the list of top suspects in the Russian Collusion story, but he is regarded by many as the most imposing of all the "victims" or "villains" of the Mueller investigation. Not that many people would get away with faulting someone for thinking that Roger Stone was partly responsible for attracting so much negative publicity onto himself, which led to his January 25, 2019 arrest and indictment on seven charges relating to five counts of lying to investigators, to witness tampering and to obstructing an official proceeding. Released on bond that same day, he pledged to fight the charges.

The sharp-tongued Roger Stone came across as an agent provocateur all right when he appeared to let the cat out of the bag by hinting on twitter about damaging information that was about to be brought to the open on Hillary Clinton and her 2016 presidential campaign chairman John Podesta. The fact that he sent out those tweets just days before October 7, 2016, which is when WikiLeaks started publishing the thousands of emails it claimed were retrieved from Podesta's private Gmail account, made it all the more logical that he found himself included in the list of top Trump campaign aides who knew about plans by WikiLeaks to release the stolen emails to the public. For the simple reason that the emails compromised Hillary Clinton's positions or campaign strategy, and the fact that they were believed to have been stolen from the Clinton campaign and Democratic National Committee by Russian operatives, Roger Stone inadvertently made himself highly suspected not only of involvement with the Russians believed to have done the hacking, but also of dealing with WikiLeaks.

A curious mind would be hard-pressed for an answer as to whether Roger Stone could be an agent-provocateur as he himself claimed; and if so what did he really mean when he said among other things that *"One man's dirty trick is another man's political, civic action."*?

There is no doubt that Roger Stone has been fighting the charges, which he considered politically motivated, in a manner that smacks of indignation. And he has been doing so vigorously and with fanfare that is worthy of attention, maintaining his claim or pledge that he would not "bear false witness" against Donald Trump, a stand that has seen him denying any wrongdoing before and after the election. That is why as he echoes the president by repeatedly calling the investigation a "witch-hunt", he is basically affirming the claim that the accusations of collusion with Russia are "a steaming plate of bull...", as he once said.

Even so, hardly anyone saw it coming when on February 18, 2019; he posted a photo on Instagram of Amy Berman Jackson, the federal judge overseeing his case, with what looked like crosshairs of a rifle scope next to the judge's head. Despite Stone's apology the next day, Amy Berman Jackson responded to the uncalled-for gaffe by imposing a full gag order on the beleaguered defendant on grounds that he would not "pose a danger" to others if he did not discuss the case in public.

When on June 20, 2019, Assistant U.S. Attorney Jonathan Kravis led other prosecutors in writing that "Stone's posts violate this Court's order that Stone not comment 'in the media or in public settings about the Special Counsel's investigation or this case or any of the participants in the investigation or the case.'", Travis came across as someone who was firmly convinced that the recent social media posts by the longtime Trump confidante attacking the FBI and Robert S. Mueller III's special counsel probe was another repeat of his violation of the federal judge's gag order. Regardless of how the different factions look at it, it is the reaction of the commentators that were most irksome to the prosecution. Not only did some of them refer to the investigation as a *"Russia Hoax"*, but some of them also went as far as applauding the Roger Stone defense team for revealing *"deeply disturbing lessons about the level of corruption at the top levels of the agencies charged with protecting us from external threats..."* Those statements are in essence are a condemnation of the intelligence community.

The flamboyant Roger Stone seems to be taking the recent developments seriously as his November 5, 2019 trial date approaches because he held a fundraiser in Annadale, a middle-class neighborhood of New York City, in Staten Island three days later, in a bid to recoup some of the $2 million in lawyer bills that the case is costing him. So when on July 16, 2019, Judge Amy Berman Jackson of the Washington, D.C., district court banned him from posting anything whatsoever on all major social media platforms (Instagram, Facebook, and Twitter) after he violated an already strict gag order in his criminal case, pundits could not help but muse about the fact that he got lucky, especially after a litany of his recent posts from his Instagram account was provided as evidence of his violation of the gag order aimed at preventing him from prejudicing future jurors.

IV: Gregory Bestor Craig

When on August 12, 2019, news reached the public announcing the August 19, 2019, trial date for Gregory Bestor Craig, a lawyer who worked as a White House Counsel from January 20, 2009 – January 3, 2010, under the administration of President Barack Obama, it marked a curious phase in American politics post-Mueller Report or what is otherwise called the Report on the Investigation into Russian Interference in the 2016 Presidential Election. As a matter of fact, Craig was highly regarded in the upper echelons of the Democratic Party owing to the fact that he served well in the Obama administration and also left a good impression working as a White House counsel in the Clinton administration from July 10, 1997 – September 16,

1998. That is why his indictment in April 2019 for withholding information from the Justice Department and for deliberately giving false information to it surprised many people.

Craig might not have found himself in hot water today had he returned to his old law firm Williams & Connolly after leaving his White House counsel job in 2010 or had he turned down the more enticing offer to work for the more renowned law firm Skadden, Arps, Slate, Meagher & Flom LLP and Affiliates, sometimes called Skadden Arps or what is commonly known as Skadden. But he would join the firm in January 2010 as the Global Policy and Litigation Strategy Practice Group partner and would carry out work for it from its Washington DC office, representing high profile clients such as Goldman Sachs and John Eduard, the Democratic nominee for Vice President in 2004.

The genesis of it all was May 2010, the day the Ukrainian General Prosecutor's office started a number of criminal cases against Yulia Tymoshenko, the pro-Western candidate who after losing the February 07, 2010 runoff of the presidential election to Yanukovych, stayed virulently opposed to the new Ukrainian president. Craig should have become wary after the European Parliament passed a resolution condemning the Yanukovych government for persecuting Tymoshenko and for its prosecution of several cases against her and her ministers, of which the "Gas case", based on a contract she signed in 2009 with the Russian gas company Gazprom to supply natural gas to Ukraine in her capacity as the Prime Minister of Ukraine, was the most prominent. The court would charge Tymoshenko with abuse of power and embezzlement on the grounds that the deal did not serve Ukraine's interest and that it was for personal benefits. This would lead to her sentencing to seven years in jail among other judgments, punishments she started serving on December 30, 2011.

Some experts hold that Craig got himself into legal trouble after he failed to register as a foreign agent in contravention of the law requiring lobbyist to do so when lobbying on behalf of foreign governments. This was following a 2012 job he did for the government of Ukraine under the presidency of Viktor Yanukovych who was derided by western-governments for his pro-Russian stance and for being responsible for the incarceration of Yulia Tymoshenko, a darling of the West and a hero of the 2004 Orange Revolution in Ukraine. Even though the Yanukovych government commissioned the team of Skadden lawyers that Craig led to look into errors in the Tymoshenko trial; and even though the report the Craig-led team produced showed that Yulia Tymoshenko was prevented from having legal counsel at "critical stages" of the court case, and from having critical witnesses summoned to enhance her defense; the report concluded that Tymoshenko's conviction was not politically motivated by Yanukovych to stifle the opposition, and that it was supported by evidence.

Craig not only failed to promote his controversial report among journalists and members of congress, he equally failed to be convincing to Tymoshenko's lawyers and human rights groups. That is why not many people were surprised when he resigned from Skadden in April 2018 after the Special Counsel investigation indicted Alex van der Zwaan, a lawyer at the firm's London office who participated in his team that carried out the investigative job on Tymoshenko's incarceration. However, many people thought the matter was settled for good after Skadden paid $4.6 million as part of a settlement with the U.S. Justice Department over unregistered work the law firm did in cooperation with Paul Manafort for the Yanukovych government. His April 2019 indictment was a surprise all right. However, it is his trial scheduled for August 19, 2019, that is going to determine the extent of the Ukraine debacle in the whole Special Counsel investigation that looks certain to reverberate for many more months or maybe even many more years to come.

V: The Russians

We are likely to miss the big picture and undermine the seriousness of the Special Counsel investigation's work on Russian interference in the 2016 United States elections and suspicious links between Trump associates and Russian officials if we fail to dwell on the Russians who were caught in the crosshairs of the Special Counsel investigation and found a spot in the Mueller report, and more especially if we focus instead or exclusively on the American actors in what is supposed to be a drama casting mother Russia as the principal villain that got its children to "defile the sacredness of US. elections by hacking into America's electoral machinery and influencing some of the actors involved in the campaigns and elections.

Even though not a single Russian citizen has been judged or sentence, most of those who have so far been indicted have been Russians. We can divide the indictees into three categories:

1. The Ukrainian-born Konstantin Kilimnik who also holds Russian citizenship following his higher education in Russia and early years working there, stands out as the most prominent Russian to be indicted by the jury of the Special Counsel investigation on charges of obstruction of justice and of conspiracy to obstruct justice by attempting to tamper with a witness on behalf of Paul Manafort. Referenced extensively by the Mueller Report, Kilimnik who worked for Manafort for more than a decade from his base in the Ukrainian capital city of Kiev is perceived to have had ties to the Russian intelligence, something he has denied repeatedly and vehemently. However, what he could not deny were his connections to Russian and Ukrainian business moguls including Oleg Deripaska, Rinat Akhmetov and Serhiy Lyovochkin. The Mueller investigation saw criminality in his business dealings with Manafort during the spring and the summer of 2018 when he supposedly served as a conduit between Manafort and interests that opposed the post-Yanukovych

American/EU-backed government in Ukraine—meaning those who opposed the former Ukrainian president Yanukovych, Russia, and pro-Russian forces in Ukraine. Kilimnik closed down on his June 8, 2018, indictment through an email exchange with the Washington Post on April 05, 2019 where he stated the following among other things: *"I have no ties to Russian or, for that matter, any intelligence operation...This is one of the biggest mistakes in the public perception and in the report. It is simply not based on any facts and is a made-up narrative...I absolutely have zero to do with the Russia interference in the U.S. elections investigated by Mr. Mueller."*

The catch, however, is that though admitting the Soviet and later Russian intelligence educated and trained him in the Moscow Military University, he also claims he was dismissed from Russia's Federal Security Service in the early 2000s.

2. Three days before President Trump met with the Russian President Vladimir V. Putin in Helsinki, Finland, the Special Investigation indicted 12 Russians considered to be intelligence agents for Russia's GRU (the foreign military-intelligence agency of the General Staff of the Armed Forces of the Russian Federation) on grounds that they hacked the Democratic National Committee and the Clinton presidential campaign. Citing a litany of brazen subterfuge operations that these agents

allegedly carried out with the intention to sow chaos shortly before November 8, 2016, the 29-page indictment presented a case against Russia that is hard for an average person to dismiss. The alleged actions carried out by the Russian agents included money laundering, phishing, and attempts to access the election board of several states in the USA. However, pro-Trump forces and Russia regarded the timing of the indictment as a well-planned effort to torpedo the July 16, 2018 Helsinki summit, the first between the two presidents, which they were hoping would thaw the developing Cold-War between Russia and the USA and its allies that was sparked off by the overthrow of Ukraine's Yanukovych, the coming to power of pro-Western forces in Ukraine, Russia's annexation of the Ukrainian province of Crimea (Soviet Russia's until 1956 when the then leader of the Soviet Union Nikita Khrushchev transferred it to the Soviet Republic of Ukraine) and the armed conflict in Ukraine's Donbass (the provinces of Lugansk and Donetsk that were the strongholds of the deposed Ukrainian president). The fact that none of the twelve Russian intelligence agents have been arraigned, especially as they live abroad, safely away from American jurisdiction, makes the verifiability of the charges against them difficult and controversial indeed. Besides, the constitution of Russia, just like that of the USA, generally shields its citizens from extradition and deportation.

That is why it is highly unlikely that any of the Russian citizens would be whisked off to the United States of America for judgment.

3. The 13 Russians and three companies indicted on February 16, 2018, for aiding the Trump Campaign are said to constitute the part of Russian interference that the Special Counsel investigation apparently does not consider a direct handiwork of Russia's intelligence services. Described as a sophisticated network that undermined targeted candidates and the American political system, the interconnection involved among other things a smooth-operating Internet Research Agency in the Russian imperial city of St. Petersburg, and is said to have stretched into the social feeds in the USA through social media campaigns aimed at picking at Americans, exacerbating their political divisions, and organizing rallies, especially in the election battleground states, all to the benefit of Donald Trump. Some of the 13 indicted Russian civilians included clients of Richard Pinedo who bought bank accounts from him over the internet. The fact that all the three indicted companies are owned by the catering business magnate Yevgeny Prigozhin, who besides being one of the 13 indictees, also happened to have hosted several dinners in Russia for foreign dignitaries that Vladimir Putin also attended, gives the whole affair a bizarre twist. Like in the other category of cases involving Russia, no

headway was expected in these charges. So when on May 08, 2019, a pair of lawyers from one of the indicted companies —Concord Management and Consulting, LLC —beat expectations by appearing at the federal court in Washington to plead not guilty to the charges, they put to question the claims by Mueller's office that the Russian government had not cooperated with their efforts to serve summonses on those indicted on charges of being involved in a relentless, well-financed and multi-pronged operation that subverted the 2016 presidential election.

Today, it is obvious the awaited verdicts on the cases involving Michael Flynn, Rick Gates and Roger Stone do not stir Americans as much as they did prior to the release of the report of the Special Counsel investigation. In the opinion of some, the Mueller Report inadvertently exonerated Donald Trump and his team of collusion with Russia, and in so doing, unwittingly weakened the case regarding the involvement of Russia and Russians in the outcome of the 2016 presidential election.

Now, the question is whether the Trump administration is going to make a winning out of its thirty months in office by drawing on its successes, mastering the tools for overcoming the challenges confronting it and Americans, building on its strengths, neutralizing the threats to it, and by capitalizing on the opportunities that it can tap successfully to carry it through the next seventeen months in such a positive manner that it would increase its chances of winning the 2020 presidential election, thereby making Donald Trump a two-term president despite the strong opposition from the president's opponents, enemies and rivals.

A Summary of those indicted by the Mueller Investigation

	NAME	CHARGES	RESULTS
	Roger Stone, Former Trump adviser	Indicted on charges of lying to Congress, obstruction and witness tampering.	Pleaded not guilty
	Michael Cohen, Former Trump attorney	False statements to Congress	Pleaded guilty; sentenced to 3 years in prison Dec. 12

	NAME	CHARGES	RESULTS
	Paul Manafort, Former Trump campaign chair	Two federal cases involving tax and bank fraud, money laundering and obstruction	7.5 years in prison; $24 million in restitution
	George Papadopoulos, Former Trump campaign aide	Lying to FBI	Pleaded guilty; sentenced to 14 days in prison.
	Michael Flynn, Former national security adviser	Lying to FBI	Pleaded guilty; sentencing delayed.
	Rick Gates, Former Trump campaign aide	Conspiracy, lying to FBI and special counsel's office	Pleaded guilty; cooperating with prosecutors.

NAME	CHARGES	RESULTS
Alex van der Zwann, Attorney	Lying to FBI	Pleaded guilty; sentenced to 30 days in prison.
Richard Pinedo, Data broker	Identity fraud	Pleaded guilty; sentenced to six months in prison.
Konstantin Kilimnik, Associate of Paul Manafort	Obstruction of justice, conspiracy to obstruct justice	
12 intelligence agents for Russia's GRU	Conspiracy to commit computer crimes, identity theft, money laundering	

	NAME	CHARGES	RESULTS
	13 Russians and three affiliated companies	Conspiracy to defraud the U.S., conspiracy to commit wire/ bank fraud, identity theft	
	Name	Charges	Result

SOURCE: Federal court filings via AP

CHAPTER FOUR

Forerunner

Cassandra (also called Alexandra) in Greek Mythology was a Trojan princess and seeress who was cursed with the powers to utter prophecies that though true were never believed by those around her, especially those the prophecies were meant to help because she was deprived of the power of persuasion. Her most notable prophecies were of her brother Paris's abduction of Helen, the Trojan War, and of the Destruction of Troy.

It is okay for the different camps in a race to convince themselves that they stand to prevail over their opponents. After all, that is the essence of competition or the reason why people and entities compete—they look forward to winning and getting the benefits of their victories. In fact, they do not just intend to win; they expect to prevail over their opponents in a manner that would dissuade their vanquished rivals from challenging them again. And as it is often the case, they wouldn't stop preparing for the day of the competition until the last minute.

Voicing fears or concerns about your opponent is often regarded as a measure of your grasp of the strength of the competitor(s) or competition you are up against. The fear could be paralyzing if you allow it to overwhelm you. However, when it comes to the true movers and shakers of this world, fear is often a motivator, the shot that would spur them out of their complacency and stir their senses, propelling them to overcome obstacles they did not imagine themselves prevailing over a short while ago. The fear then strengthens them; the fear becomes a strength, a channel to knowledge. After all, didn't Sun Tzu, the ancient but famous Chinese general, military strategist, writer and philosopher, articulate the importance of knowing your enemy in his memorable book "The Art of War", when he wrote among other things that "*If you know the enemy and know yourself, you need not fear the result of a hundred battles.*"?

That is why when elements of the left-wing media, especially those that earned a reputation over the years for being virulently against the 45th president of the United States of America, voiced concerns that explicitly or implicitly told their audiences that they too think Donald Trump has a high chance of winning the 2020 presidential election unless something dramatic happens, we are expected to take them seriously. Some may see these peculiar anti-Trumpists echoing those sentiments as messengers of doom, not knowing that there are others who discern something more complex in the statements of the supposed doomsayers. These questioning anti-Trump people see knowledge, if not wisdom being circulated by the "Cassandrists" in the media. In a way, the anti-Trump media echoing those seemingly negative views are indeed cautioning the Democratic hopefuls and the Democratic Party in general not to underestimate the man they have been hounding over the past four years in the hope of disarraying him.

As a matter of fact, a March 22, 2019 article by Vox.com echoed that sentiment through its first paragraph that read thus: *"For Democrats, there is one big fear heading into the 2020 election: A booming economy could save Donald Trump."*

However, it is Goldman Sach's June 25, 2019 article favoring Donald Trump to win reelection in 2020 that raises eyebrows. Entitled *"The Goldman Sachs Trump Chart That Should Scare Democrats Right Now"*, it expatiated on the Vox.com article by using the Gross Domestic Product (GDP) matrix, which though not the complete measure of economic well-being of a country, has correlated closely with past election wins in the USA when the economy is not shrinking or stagnating, and more especially when the GDP growth is good. The Goldman Sachs article was succinct in its prediction or caution when it wrote that: *"More to the point is that the economy could weaken before election time. But Goldman's 2.2% growth estimate already represents a slowdown from last year's 2.9%. It still might be just enough."*

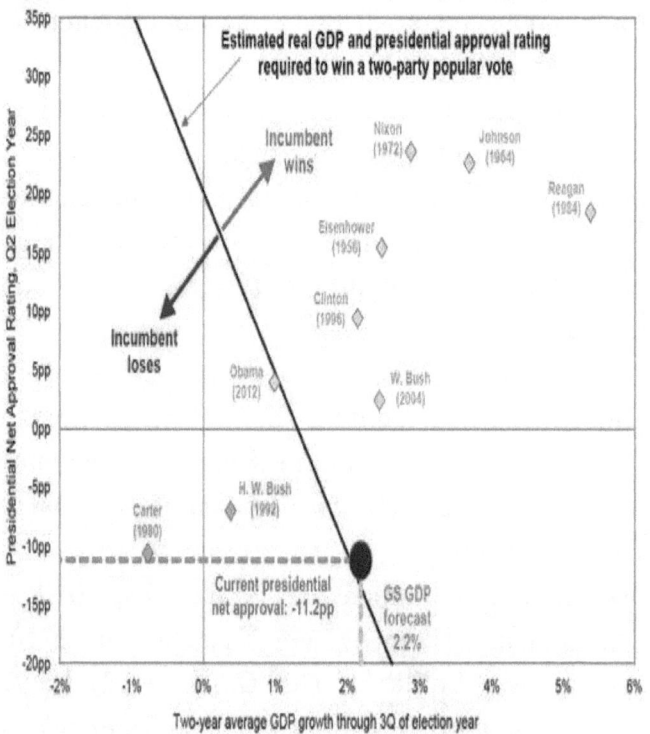

Economic growth forecast suggests popular vote victory for President Trump possible despite negative net approval rating

It is not difficult to understand why the American multinational investment bank and financial services company had to dwell so much on the economy. It is a business entity, and as such, it thrives on a robust economy because a booming economy is good for businesses. That is why Goldman Sachs sees an inevitable Trump victory in 2020 if the presidential election is contested chiefly on the back of the economy. However, there are other factors Donald Trump can harness to win the 2020 presidential election in spite of the economy or in addition to it. One of them has more to do with psychology than anything else. Incumbents have a 2 to 1 chance of winning reelection as the table below clearly shows. However, incumbency and the advantages it carries with it is not something to dwell on in this chapter. We shall look at the things that make the United States of America tick and how Donald Trump is taking advantage of them to win the 2020 race for the White House.

Regions of the USA

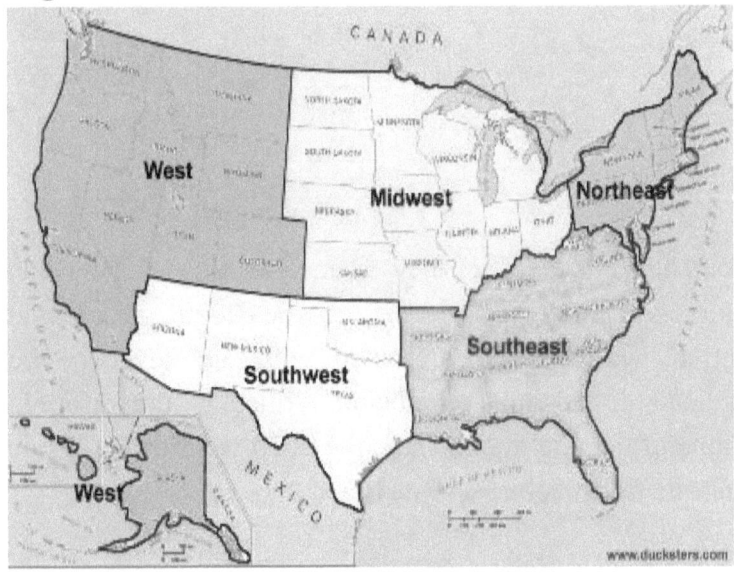

TABLE 2

Has the Party Holding the Presidency Kept It?[a]

Elections with an Incumbent Candidate Running	
Yes, Kept the Presidency (N = 21)	No, Lost the Presidency (N = 10)
1792 Washington	1800 J. Adams lost to Jefferson
1804 Jefferson	1828 J.Q. Adams lost to Jackson
1812 Madison	1840 Van Buren lost to W.H. Harrison
1820 Monroe	1888 Cleveland lost to B. Harrison
1832 Jackson	1892 B. Harrison lost to Cleveland
1864 Lincoln	1912 Taft lost to Wilson
1872 Grant	1932 Hoover lost to F.D. Roosevelt
1900 McKinley	1976 Ford lost to Carter
1904 T. Roosevelt	1980 Carter lost to Reagan
1916 Wilson	1992 G.H.W. Bush lost to Clinton
1924 Coolidge	
1936 F.D. Roosevelt	
1940 F. D. Roosevelt	
1944 F.D. Roosevelt	
1948 Truman	
1956 Eisenhower	
1964 L.B. Johnson	
1972 Nixon	
1984 Reagan	
1996 Clinton	
2004 G.W. Bush	

In our hand in hand journey to analyze those factors that would determine the results of the 2020 presidential election, we shall be presented with the never before fathomed threads that are being refined in the different regions of the country to make the 2020 race for the White House the most colorful of its time.